How to Improve Your Reading Comprehension

BY BERTHA DAVIS AND SUSAN WHITFIELD

A Language Skills Concise Guide

FRANKLIN WATTS

New York | London | Toronto | Sydney | 1980

Illustrations by Vantage Art, Inc.

Cartoon on p. 64 by Lafe Locke appeared previously in the March 5, 1977, issue of *Saturday Review*. Reprinted by permission of the artist. Excerpt on regeneration, pp. 17 to 18, adapted from "The Miracle of Regeneration: Can Human Limbs Grow Back?" by Susan Schiefelbein, which appeared in the July 8, 1979 issue of *Saturday Review*. Reprinted by permission of the publisher. Excerpt on bees, pp. 50 to 51, reprinted by permission of The New York Times Company, © 1979. Excerpt on seriousness, pp. 52 to 53, taken from "The Back Door" in the September 2, 1978 issue of *Saturday Review*. Reprinted by permission of the publisher.

Library of Congress Cataloging in Publication Data

Davis, Bertha, 1910–
How to improve your reading comprehension.

(A Language skills concise guide)
Includes index.
1.   Reading comprehension—Juvenile literature.
I.   Whitfield, Susan, joint author.
II.   Title.   III.   Series:
Language skills concise guide.
LB1050.45.D38   428.4′3   80–14693
ISBN 0–531–04132–8

Contents

Chapter I.
Get the Message
1

Chapter II.
Watch the Signals
15

Chapter III.
Make Purpose Central
26

Chapter IV.
Keep Your Eye on the Forest
41

Chapter V.
Take Tests in Stride
56

Index
68

Chapter I.
Get the Message

Every sentence you read was written to give you a message. If you get the message, you comprehend the sentence. If no message is received, you are not comprehending.

What is a sentence? Not all groups of words are sentences. A group of words is a sentence only if it carries a message. To carry a message, a group of words must

name a person, place, or thing—the CORE SUBJECT of the sentence

and

tell what the core subject did or is doing or will do

or

tell the state of being of the core subject. The words that do this make up the CORE VERB of the sentence.

The boat. Is this a sentence? Of course it isn't. The words give you no message.

Sank. Is this a sentence? Of course it isn't. The word gives you no message.

The long, graceful boat, its sails damaged by the violent wind, its prow rising and dipping dangerously low into the enormous waves.

Is this a sentence? Be careful with this one! You have a core subject, clearly enough—a boat. And you have a lot of descriptive information about the boat. But there is no core verb to tell you what the boat did, is doing, or will do. There is no message. Maybe the boat fought its way to a safe harbor. Maybe it sank.

The boat sank. Is this a sentence? It certainly is. You have a core subject, and you have a core verb that tells you what the core subject did. There is a message.

Core subject and core verb—these are the keys that unlock sentences. Find them, and everything else in the sentence falls into place. Miss them, and you miss the message of the sentence.

Short, simple sentences present no problem. But textbooks, newspapers, magazine articles, works of literature, and reading comprehension tests, of course, are not a series of short, easy sentences. There will be times when you move through a group of words, come to the period that marks the end of the group, and find yourself thinking, "What in the world did that say?" This chapter will give you some attack strategies to help you figure out the messages that are buried in long, complicated sentences.

The first step in unlocking a complicated sentence is to find the core subject—the person or thing the message is about. Look at the four sentences below. In which way are they alike—in length, in the subject with which they deal, or in punctuation?

(A) Tugboats on the Mississippi threatened to come to a halt when fuel prices began to soar.

(B) A knowledge of fish sounds can avoid confusion and unneeded effort when a new sound is picked up and the sound sentry must decide whether or not to call an alert.

(C) The recent advances in understanding gene function and expression stem largely from the new and sometimes controversial technology called recombinant DNA research.

(D) The Chief Librarian and his staff have devoted their lives to making the four million or more books and pamphlets serve the public to a degree that cannot be approached by any similar great institution in the Old World.

You can readily see that the sentences differ in length and in subject. But they are alike in the fact that they contain only one punctuation mark apiece—a period at the end of the sentence.

Which sentence is about the Chief Librarian and his staff? Which is about a knowledge of fish sounds? Which is about Mississippi tugboats? Which is about advances in the understanding of gene function? Why is it so easy to match these sentences with their subjects? Because the core subject of each sentence appears at the beginning of the sentence.

It is usually unsound to generalize from as few as four examples. But these examples were specially chosen so you would notice a fact that is generally true about sentences that have no commas within them. The core subject of such sentences always appears in the first few words of the sentence. So here is one strategy for untangling long sentences: When a sentence is uninterrupted by a comma you can be pretty sure that the first person, place, or thing named in the sentence is the core subject of the sentence—the subject the message deals with.

With the core subject identified, your second task is clear. Find an *action* word that tells you what the core subject did, is doing, or will do. Or, find a *state-of-being* word that tells you what state or condition the core subject is in, was in, or will be in.

Here is a word of caution about core verbs. An action word ending in *-ing* cannot be a core verb unless there is a state-of-being verb with it. *Is, are, was, were, will be, has been,* and *had been* are state-of-being verbs.

The boy playing. This is not a sentence. What did the playing boy do?

> The boy is playing.
> The boy was playing.
> The boy has been playing.

All these groups of words send messages. They are sentences.

Look again at Sentence (B) on page 2. What can a *knowledge of fish sounds* do? It *can avoid.* Now you have found the core verb. With this, plus the core subject of the sentence picked out, everything else makes sense.

Now go one step further. Look at the core subject and core verb together and ask yourself, "What can a knowledge of fish sounds avoid?" Your eye moves further along the sentence and you see that the answer is *confusion and unneeded effort.*

What job do all the other words in Sentence (B) do? They describe a situation in which a knowledge of fish sounds would avoid confusion—*when a new sound is picked up and the sound sentry must decide whether or not to call an alert.*

After working with Sentence (B), you should be able to answer a question such as this:

Choose the best ending for this sentence:

When the sound sentry picks up a new sound, he or she must always (a) report confusion and unneeded effort, (b) use his or her knowledge, (c) sound an alert, or (d) learn about basic fish sounds.

You chose (b) didn't you? If you did, you were right.

Let's turn to Sentence (C) on pages 2 to 3. When you found in that sentence that the message was about *advances,* the core verb had to be *stem—advances stem.* You've got that, so you ask yourself, "Stem from what?" And you see that the rest of the words in that sentence answer your question.

Sentence (D) on page 3 is equally straightforward when you look for a core verb that makes sense with *The Chief Librarian and his staff. Have devoted* tells you what they did. "Devoted what?" you ask yourself. The words *their lives* answer that question and raise another: "Devoted their lives to what?" The rest of the words in the sentence do two jobs. They tell you what the staff tried to do, and they tell you how well they did that job compared to the job done by other librarians.

Now sort out this sentence using the core subject-core verb strategy:

A considerable portion of the improvement in telephone sound is attributable to practical applications of laboratory investigations concerning the mechanisms of human speech and audition.

You can readily see that the message is about *a considerable part of the improvement in telephone sound.* You can see that *is attributable* would make sense as a state-of-being verb linked to your core subject. *Improvement is attributable* makes you ask yourself, "Attributable to what?" Your question is the clue to the job done by the rest of the words in the sentence. They must tell you what caused the improvement. What is there in the remaining words that would explain improvement in sound? Your eye lights on *applications of laboratory investigations.* You mentally ask, "Investigations into what?" and you immediately see that the investigations dealt with how people talk and how they listen.

Sometimes you are asked to demonstrate your understanding of a complicated sentence by filling in a missing word in a sentence that follows the complicated sentence. Here is a sentence that followed the sentence you have just worked on. From the choices given, mentally choose the one which proves that you understood the long sentence.

These _____ have exerted a profound influence.
(a) studies   (b) rates
(c) materials   (d) machines   (e) companies

How could the missing word be anything but *studies*?

The clue to untangling the complicated sentences you have dealt with thus far in this chapter lay in noting that they contained no commas. In fact commas are clues to untangling almost any long, difficult sentence you meet. Writers use commas for precisely that purpose—to help readers find their way efficiently through long sentences. Why, you might ask, don't they just write short, direct sentences? Why don't they always put the core subject up front where you can't miss it? Style, that's why. They want sentences that flow, not bump along. One straightforward message after another can sound very unpleasant.

There are patterns to sentences, however, and you can learn to use these patterns. Take one-comma sentences, for example, of which there are several kinds. The following sentence, illustrating one kind of one-comma sentence, should cause you no trouble.

He has a low, pleasant voice.

This use of the comma—to separate words in a series—you have known since third grade.

Other kinds of one-comma sentences sometimes take a little thinking. To make that thinking easier, here are two sentence patterns. Almost every one-comma sentence you meet will follow one of them.

PATTERN A
It was a beautiful house, and they fell in love with it.
It was a beautiful house, but it was not what they needed.

PATTERN B
Judging from the style and construction of the house, they
    decided it was about two hundred years old.

Pattern A sentences are easy. There are *always* two messages in sentences like these. So, to grasp their meaning quickly, first find the core subject and core verb in the words *before* the comma. Then find the core subject and core verb in the words *after* the comma. You will always end up with two messages, and they will always be closely related to each other. In *and* sentences, the second message usually supports or extends the first message. In *but* sentences, the relationship is different in two important ways: (1) the second message contrasts with or changes the first message, and (2) the message after *but* is usually the one the author wants to emphasize. *But* is an especially useful word to writers. You will read more about it in Chapter II.

For Pattern B sentences you must take a different approach. First, read the words *after* the comma. Is a person, place, or thing named straightaway? Are there action or state-of-being words that make sense when linked with that person, place, or thing? Then you have found the core subject and core verb of the whole sentence. Watch out! A person, place, or thing may not be named right after the comma. But is there a pronoun—*she, he, it, they*? If there is, then that pronoun is the core subject of the whole sentence. Just go back to the words before the comma to find the pronoun's antecedent, the one or more words *she, he, it,* or *they* refer to.

With the core of the message pinned down, you won't have much trouble figuring out what job the before-the-comma words do in a sentence.

If a person, place, thing, or referring pronoun does not appear *right after* the comma in a Pattern B sentence, you can be pretty sure that the core subject and core verb of the sentence message are *before* the comma. Go back and look for them. When they are pinned down, the after-the-comma words will fall into place.

Now try using the strategies suggested above to untangle the sentences that follow. They have been broken up to encourage you to think about them in pieces, as the strategies suggest. After each of these practice sentences there is a checkup sentence. If you can correctly complete the checkup sentence, then you will have successfully untangled the practice sentence. You will have *comprehended* it. Write your answers on a separate sheet of paper.

Igneous rocks compose	*but*	they are generally covered
the greater part of the		at the surface by a relatively
earth's crust,		thin layer of sedimentary or
		metamorphic rocks.

So we ———— see them.
(a) never   (b) generally
(c) often   (d) seldom   (e) barely

When you looked at this comma-*but* sentence, you knew there were two messages. You readily found the core subject (*igneous rocks*) and the core verb (*compose*) of the first message. You recognized *they* as the core subject of the second message, and your common sense told you that the look-for-antecedent strategy works here too. So the core subject and core verb of the second message were *igneous rocks* and *are covered.* The other words of the sentence told (1) the extent to which they are covered—*generally*—and (2) by what they are covered—*a relatively thin layer of sedimentary or metamorphic rocks.* If the igneous rocks are generally covered, how often will you see them? Following this line of reasoning you would know that the checkup sentence has to read, "So we seldom see them," (d).

Regarding physical changes that have been and are now taking place on the surface of the earth, the sea and its shores have been the scene of the greatest stability.

No new _____ are in our future.
(a) deserts   (b) mountains
(c) rivers   (d) oceans   (e) volcanoes

In this Pattern B sentence, the message is that *the sea and its shores have been the scene of the greatest stability.* So the sea and its shores are least likely to produce something new. This line of reasoning should lead you to complete the checkup sentence with the word *oceans,* (d).

With the use of electronic instruments and earth satellites, enormous gains have taken place recently in identifying and tracking storms over regions that have but few meteorological stations.

Even while the storm is passing high above a(n) _____, we can follow it.
(a) generator   (b) spaceship
(c) ocean   (d) meteorologist   (e) barometer

(9)

In this Pattern B sentence, the core subject *enormous gains* and the core verb *have taken place* should have made you ask, "Gains in what?" And the answer to that question should have led you directly to choice (c), the only choice that is a *region* with *few meteorological stations.*

Bell's original electro-magnetic telephone transmitter functioned likewise as a receiver, the same instrument being held alternately to mouth and ear.

But having to ———— the instrument
this way was inconvenient.
(a) store (b) use
(c) test (d) strip (e) clean

Here did you avoid the trap in the words following the comma by recalling that an *-ing* word can only be a core verb when preceded by *is, are, was,* etc.? If you did, then you knew that the message was in the words *before* the comma. The words after the comma simply answered your mental question, "How could it function as a receiver as well as a transmitter?" This took you to the correct answer, choice (b).

Combination handsets *but* prospects for their acceptance were produced for commercial utilization late in the nineteenth century, prospects for their acceptance were uncertain as the initial quality of transmissions with the handsets was disappointing.

But ———— transmissions followed.
(a) shorter (b) fewer
(c) better (d) faster (e) cheaper

The two messages in this comma-*but* sentence untangle into

handsets produced   (but)   prospects were uncertain

The remaining words of the first message tell (1) the purpose for which they were produced—for sale—and (2) when they were produced—late in the nineteenth century. The remaining words of the second message tell the reason for the disappointing prospects—disappointing quality. Since the checkup sentence begins with *But,* you look for a contrasting or modifying word to go with *transmissions.* The clearest contrast to *disappointing quality* is choice (c).

We could go on and on with sentence patterns, but for untangling sentences that contain two or more commas or sentences with semicolons or dashes, we will simply give you one general strategy. That strategy, of course, is to help you find the core subject and core verb. Once you have these pinned down, you can easily figure out what function all the other words in the sentence serve.

Step 1. Break up the troublesome sentence into the groups of words created by the punctuation. Handle groups of words separated by semicolons as if they were separate sentences.

Step 2. Ignore, for the present, any groups of words within dashes and any group of words that starts with a little word such as *who, which, where, if, to, as, while, when, because, since, though,* and *although.* These little words always signal "Here is a *detail* of time, place, identification, cause, or comparison."

Step 3. Starting with the first group of words that is left, look for the name of the person, place, thing, or referring pronoun that could be the core subject. Then look for an action or a state-of-being word that would make sense when linked with that core subject. With these two pinned down, you can begin to ask yourself the questions that will reveal the function of all the other words in the sentence.

Now try using the strategy to untangle the sentences that follow. They have been broken up as the strategy suggests. After each sentence is a question with which you can test yourself to see whether or not you got the message. Write your answers on a separate sheet of paper.

While gaso-line lines were getting headline attention, inflation— a far greater threat to the average person— quietly continued to worsen.

Which is the core verb: (a) were getting, (b) continued, or (c) to worsen? If you chose (b), you successfully followed the steps of the strategy. You ignored the *while* group of words, so *were getting* could not be the core verb. You ignored *a greater threat to the average person* because it was a group of words within dashes. You looked among the words that were left for the name of a person, place, thing, or referring pronoun, and found *inflation.* Then you looked for an action or a state-of-being word that made sense when linked to *inflation* and found *continued.*

When we look for causes of events, however, we must not make the mistake of assuming that just because one event preceded another, it caused the second event.

Which is the core subject: (a) causes, (b) we, (c) mistake, (d) it, or (e) event? *Causes* could not be the core subject because it appears in the group of words beginning with *when,* and you ignored that group, right? *We* is the first person, place, thing, or referring pronoun that is named in the groups of words you should examine. So you look for action or state-of-being words that would make sense when linked to *we.* You immediately see that *must not make* would make sense, so you know you have the core subject and core verb. "We must not make what?" you ask. "The mistake," you say. "What mistake?" you ask. "The mistake of assuming that. . . ." With the sentence untangled in this way you can easily complete a checkup sentence like this:

Such a(n) —————— is
very likely to be sheer accident.
(a) sequence   (b) reasoning
(c) error   (d) cause   (e) argument

Sequence (a) is the word that makes sense.

To keep river vessels moving freely,	bridges are built high enough,	when possible,	to let them pass underneath.

How would you complete the checkup sentence?

This solution to the problem of river traffic
does not work for very —————— ships.
(a) slow   (b) tall   (c) fast
(d) low   (e) old-fashioned

If you correctly untangled the original sentence, you know that *tall* is the only word that makes sense.

Dr. Tester's groups,	which con- ducted their experiments with both captive sharks held in large,	seminatural ponds,	and free sharks in- habiting the lagoon of Eniwetok Atoll,
found that for some sharks,	and on some occasions,	human sweat contains a component that can function as a shark repellent.	

Which word would make sense in the checkup sentence that follows?

> But it is small comfort to a
> nervous bather to know that _____
> sharks will leave him or her alone.
> (a) captive   (b) free
> (c) some   (d) no   (e) large

If you chose (c), you correctly untangled the original sentence and got its message.

At the beginning of this chapter, we said we would give you some "attack strategies" to help you figure out the messages buried in long, complicated sentences. Do you see now why the word "attack" is appropriate? To improve your reading comprehension, you must take the offensive. You don't just let words roll over you. There are messages there —a message in each sentence, an overall message in each paragraph. If those messages elude you at first, you do not give up. You attack those words and force them to yield up their message.

Chapter II.
Watch the Signals

Authors want you to comprehend what they write. You met this idea in the last chapter as you worked with sentences in which the author's punctuation helped you to untangle the message. In this chapter you will see how writers help you handle three other reading comprehension hurdles: word meanings, time relationships, and idea relationships.

WORD MEANINGS

When writers use a word that they know will not be familiar to some of their readers, they usually give the meaning of the word.

A newspaper columnist, for example, in analyzing current money and credit problems, wanted to convey this message:

Many bankers were puzzled last week
by a sharp increase in the float.

The writer was aware that although his readers would know what *float* means in relation to water, they might not know what it means in a money and banking context. So he decided to tell them. But because he wanted a smooth writing style and did not want to emphasize that he knew something they didn't, he avoided this:

> Many bankers were puzzled last week
> by a sharp increase in the float.
> Float means. . . .

Instead he wrote this:

> Many bankers were puzzled by the sharp
> increase in the float—uncollected
> checks in the process of transfer from
> bank to bank—that occurred last week.

The dashes were the writer's signal to the reader, "Here is the meaning of the word I have just used." Parentheses are sometimes used in the middle of a sentence for the same meaning-insertion purpose.

The following illustrates another definition signal:

> The library's collection of hagiology,
> literature dealing with the lives
> and works of the saints, is probably
> the most extensive in the world.

Do you see how the author signaled that he was giving you the definition of hagiology? He placed the definition between commas, immediately following the difficult word.

And here is a third way writers tell you that a definition has been supplied for you.

> When moist air blowing across the country
> reaches a mountain, it is forced to rise, is
> cooled as it rises, and drops its moisture.
> This orographic rainfall. . . .

What signaled, "Look back at what you have just read for the meaning of orographic rainfall"? The word *This* linked the definition with the technical term that followed.

TIME RELATIONSHIPS

Time or sequence relationships are important in dealing with many subjects. To make these relationships clear, writers use a special vocabulary that includes words such as *before, while, as, has, after, then, meanwhile, no longer,* and *previously.* These are simple words, but the reader must be alert to their significance. Used as signals, they will lead you through even the most complex time or sequence relation-. ships. Take this passage, for example:

(1) For centuries people have watched in wonder as salamanders regenerated (grew back) limbs that had been cut off. No one ever imagined that complicated human parts could grow back in such a way. But in recent years scientists have discovered that animals that cannot regenerate naturally can be made to do so artificially. Dr. Robert Becker has already applied newly discovered principles of regeneration to successfully treat broken human bones that had previously failed to heal even after extensive surgical procedures.

(2) Years of research have led to our present understanding of regeneration. Back in the 1700s scientists discovered that every time a creature is injured an electrical charge is produced at the site of the injury. In 1958 Dr. Becker explored this phenomenon by comparing a salamander (which can regenerate naturally) and a frog (which cannot regenerate naturally).

(3) He cut off a leg from each animal and measured the electrical current at the points of injury. On the day the legs were amputated, both creatures generated the same amount of current. But then the similarity ended. As the frog's wound scarred over, the electrical current declined to zero. Meanwhile the current in the salamander's wound switched from positive to negative and only then began to decline, reaching zero when his leg had completely grown back.

(4) Dr. Vladimirovic Polezhaev applied regeneration principles in an interesting experiment using dogs. He cut away the scar tissue from the hearts of dogs who had suffered severe heart attacks before the experiment. Soon every one of the hearts regenerated and less than five percent of the dogs died.

(5) How has the rest of the scientific community responded to these revolutionary experiments? The reaction can be summed up by this remark by Dr. Becker: "They no longer march out of my lectures."

The above passage makes it clear that writers do not always tell you about events, or steps in a sequence, in the order in which they occurred. But they are always careful to write in signals that will enable a reader to get the actual order straight.

See if you can use the signals the author of this passage provided. Go back to paragraph (1). Using the words *had previously* and *after* as clues, put the following events in the order in which they occurred. Write your answers on a separate sheet of paper.

A. The doctor applied regeneration principles to treat broken bones.

B. The bones failed to heal.

C. Extensive surgical procedures were used to treat broken bones.

Had previously told you that B occurred before A. *After* told you that C occurred before B. The correct sequence is C, B, A.

Now try paragraph (3). Use *as, only then, when,* and *meanwhile* to put these events in the order in which they occurred. Write your answers on a separate sheet of paper.

A. The salamander and frog generated the same current.

B. The similarity ended.

C. The frog's wound scarred over.

D. The frog's current declined to zero.

E. The salamander's current switched from positive to negative.

F. The salamander's current began to decline.

G. The salamander's current reached zero.

H. The salamander's leg grew completely back.

Then told you that A came before B. *As* told you that C and D occurred at the same time. *Meanwhile* told you that E was going on at the same time as C and D. *Only then* told you that E occurred before F. *When* told you that G and H occurred at the same time. The correct sequence is A, B, C/D/E, F, G/H.

Look now at paragraph (4). Using the words *before* and *soon,* put these events in the order in which they occurred. Write your answers on a separate sheet of paper.

A. He cut away tissue from dogs' hearts.

B. The dogs suffered heart attacks.

C. Almost all the hearts regenerated.

The correct sequence is B, A, C.

And finally, in relation to paragraph (5): How did the scientific community respond at first to Dr. Becker's startling discoveries? What time signal told you that the situation today is different from the way it once was? Did you say that scientists used to walk out on his lectures? Did you use the *no longer* time signal? Then you were right.

IDEA RELATIONSHIPS

We turn now to the way writers help their readers over a third reading comprehension hurdle—the connectives they use to signal idea relationships.

When you read a sentence that starts like, "I like Harry but. . . ." you can guess what's coming next—something about Harry the writer does not like, the words "he doesn't like me," or the words "nobody else does." What word told you how the second idea in the sentence would be related to the first idea? *But,* of course.

But signals: "Here comes something that will upset, challenge, question, or offer a contrast to what has gone before." Try using the *but* signal to get the meaning of this paragraph, which is from an American history textbook:

> Do you believe in freedom of religion? Chances are that you, like anyone anywhere in the United States, would answer "yes" to that question. Chances are also that the question would surprise anyone in the United States. People in this country take it for granted that they can practice any religion they wish—or none at all. That belief, like belief in government by the people, is part of the American way of life. But this was not always so.

The word *But* in the final sentence should have helped you

to clearly see this contrast in ideas:

In this country we take	But	people in this country
for granted that		did not always take
people should have		for granted that there
religious freedom.		should be religious
		freedom.

In fact signals: "Here comes something that supports or expands on the idea just before it." When you come to the third sentence in the paragraph below, stop reading after the *In fact* beginning. What idea do you think the author is going to strengthen or expand on in some way?

People should have some control over government —that was an idea Englishmen brought to America with them. People should be free to worship as they please or not at all—that was *not* an English idea. In fact, the idea of freedom of religion just did not exist anywhere in Europe at the time the American colonies were being settled.

Can you see the relationship in the sentences below?

There was no religious	In fact	there was no re-
freedom in England at		ligious freedom in
the time the settlers		*any* country in
came to America.		Europe.

So signals: "Here comes something that happened as a *result* of the fact the author just gave you."

Another small step toward religious freedom was taken in Maryland. In the early days of that colony a law was passed allowing freedom of worship to all Christians. So. . . .

What is coming? *So* signals that you must look for a *result* of the Maryland law and here it is:

So Catholics, at least, were free to practice their religion in Maryland as they could not in most of New England.

Although or *though* and *while* are other signals of idea relationships. They alert you to an unexpected or unusual connection between two facts that the writer is giving you. According to the sentence below, what did Roger Williams do? What was strange about his actions?

Roger Williams was one such man ahead of his time. Although he was a minister in the Massachusetts Bay Colony, he sharply criticized Puritan religious views.

However is the same kind of signal as *but.* The text quoted above goes on with a paragraph about the spread of the idea of religious freedom. Then follows a paragraph that begins with the word *However.* What should you be ready for: (1) additional examples of spreading religious freedom or (2) something about places or people who did *not* accept that idea? The second choice is correct, of course. If the writer planned to go on with more examples, he would have chosen a word like *furthermore* or *moreover* to signal, "Here comes more of the same."

Yet and *on the other hand* signal: "Here comes something that is a *contrast* to what has just gone before." What other two words signal this same relationship between ideas? *But* and *however,* of course.

If it were signals: "Here are two ideas that are linked in a negative fact/result relationship. The result will come about only if the fact is true. But the fact is *not* true."

> If the situation were an emergency,
> Sam would leave immediately.

Contrary to, it is not, it is a common misconception that, it was previously believed, and similar phrases give this signal: "Here comes a statement that is being dismissed; a correct statement will follow."

> It is not tooth decay but gum disease that
> generally causes loss of teeth in the elderly.

What idea is being dismissed here? Does a correct idea follow within the sentence? What is it? Did you see that *tooth decay generally causes loss of teeth in the elderly* is dismissed? Did you see that *gum disease generally causes loss of teeth in the elderly* is the correct idea?

> It is a commonly held misconception
> that the energy crisis is not real.

What do you expect to follow: (1) Evidence indicating that the energy crisis is not real? (2) Discussion of the energy-crisis-is-not-real point of view, followed by evidence indicating that the energy crisis *is* real? (3) Evidence that the energy crisis is real? Either choice (2) or choice (3) could logically follow the sentence quoted. Choice (1) would be inconsistent with the wording of that sentence.

If you train yourself to respond to these signals of idea relationships, your comprehension of textbooks, newspapers, magazine articles, and the like will grow amazingly. You will find use of these signals valuable, too, in situations other than doing assignments or reading for information. They will help you in reading comprehension tests, for example.

Here's a typical reading comprehension question, one in which you must fill the blank with one of the given words. Write your answer on a separate sheet of paper.

Despite the _____ of the critics
the book became a best-seller.

The words to choose from are: raves,
sincerity, acclaim, criticism, enthusiasm.

Despite sends you this signal: "Choose the word that would have *kept* the book from being a success." If you chose *criticism,* you were correct.

Here is a question in which you are asked to fill *two* blanks with a choice from given *pairs* of words. Write your answers on a separate sheet of paper.

The history of painting reveals
two lines of development
sometimes _____ and yet
remaining essentially _____.

The pairs to choose from are:
(a) varied and different
(b) separate and distinct
(c) clashing and incompatible
(d) merged and separate
(e) synthesized and harmonious.

Yet sends you this signal: "Choose the pair that contains words most clearly *opposite* in meaning so there will be a *contrast* in the sentence." If you chose *merged and separate,* you were correct.

Here is a question in which heeding the *but* signal will lead you to a correct choice. The sentence given is:

Space technology gives us the potential for visiting other planets, but its military role is just as revolutionary.

Heeding the *but* signal, you read the sentence this way:

Space technology   gives   potential for visiting
                                          other planets
                          but
space technology's   just as revolutionary.
military role   is

With the sentence comprehended in this way, the following related question presents no problem at all:

The author feels that in wartime space technology may play a role that (1) is greater than the role it played in space travel, (2) is as great as its role in space travel, (3) is less important than the one it played in space travel, (4) insures victory, (5) will take us to the outermost planets.

If you chose (2), you were correct.
    Very useful, are they not, these crucial connective signals?

Chapter III.
Make Purpose Central

Readers A and B are reading the same article in a science magazine. Which reader, do you think, has a better chance of getting the most out of the article?

Readers who read with a purpose get more out of what they read. They know what to look for while reading.

Now look at pages 28–29. Who do you think will get more out of reading the article there, Reader B or Reader C?

Probably you have easily recognized that Reader C's purpose was more useful than Reader B's. But why? What is the difference between them? Both readers began with an overall purpose. But as Reader C moved through the article she formed more *specific* reading purposes.

How did she do this? She used signals provided by the author. In this chapter you will learn several of these signals.

Much of the reading you do probably consists of homework assignments from textbooks. Homework reading done with purpose is far more effective than reading that merely "covers" the pages. So we will start by calling your attention to the features built into most textbooks, features that help you to form specific reading purposes.

You can get a good idea of what to look for in a reading assignment by previewing the chapter, or assigned pages,

READER A

READER B

READER B

READER C

before beginning to read. Look back at how Readers B and C began to read their magazine article. What signals did they use to form the reading purpose, "I will read to find out how rabies can be prevented"? They used:

A. The title of the magazine, *Science Today*
B. The date of the issue, May 12, 1979
C. The title of the article, "Rabies Prevention"

Always begin a textbook reading assignment by turning the title of the chapter into a reading purpose. Your purpose might be a statement, like Reader B's and Reader C's, or it might be a question like, "How can rabies be prevented?" The important point is to use the title to start thinking about *what to look for* when you begin reading.

Textbook authors take advantage of the fact that a title can help to focus reading purpose. They divide the information of each chapter into sections. Each section deals with a major part of the overall topic the chapter is about. And over each of these sections is a subtitle, or heading. An important part of a preview is a look at the headings in the chapter. If you turn each of these headings into a reading purpose before beginning to read, you are sure to be watching out for the major points in the chapter.

Suppose that in previewing a history chapter you come across these headings: "The 1850s from the Northern Point of View" and "The 1850s from the Southern Point of View." How can you use them to form one or more reading purposes to guide reading of the sections below these headings? Which of these purposes are appropriate?

A. "I will read to find out how the South viewed events before 1850."
B. "I will read to find out what events were being viewed by the North and the South during the 1850s."

C. "I will read to find contrasts between the North's and the South's point of view."

Sometimes section headings suggest more than one useful reading purpose. In this case, purposes B and C would alert you to the main points of both sections. A reading purpose like C, looking for contrasts, is especially useful. With this reading purpose you would do more than watch out for the main points. You would sort them out and organize them in order to better understand and remember them.

Chapter titles and section headings, like those listed below, suggest forming reading purposes in a different way:

"Summer Sun and Thermals"
"The Legacy of the New Deal"
"Radiosondes and Satellites"
"Debts and Reparations"

Can you define *reparations, radiosondes,* or *thermals*? Do you know what the New Deal was? Since these words appear in titles or headings you can be sure that they are important. So an unfamiliar word in a title or heading should be turned into a reading purpose. "I will read to find out what reparations means" would be one very useful purpose to guide reading of the section following the final heading listed above.

Other features of a textbook that help you establish reading purposes are the pictures, graphics, and maps that have been included to accompany the written text. If you study each illustration before beginning to read and turn each one into a reading purpose, it will help direct your attention to important points in the text.

In looking over the pictures with people in them, ask yourself, "Who are these people?" "What are they doing?" "Why are they important in the development of the chapter?"

In studying maps take note if some areas are colored differently from others. This indicates that the areas are being compared in some way. Ask yourself, "How are the areas different?" Are there arrows on the map? Ask yourself, "Who or what is moving and why?" Later, when you are reading the text, you will be watching out for the answers to your questions. In studying the graphics, notice what is being compared in each one. You might say to yourself, "It looks as if immigration to the United States increased sharply during the 1880s. There must be some reason for this." Later, in reading the text, you can check out what that reason was.

You may be surprised by how greatly your reading comprehension and retention of textbook material improve when you follow these strategies *before* you read. The rest of this chapter leaves the special world of textbooks to deal with strategies for forming and re-forming reading purposes as you read *anything.* Use them with textbooks, too, of course. But these are strategies to make *all* your reading more purposeful and your levels of reading comprehension higher.

You know that printed material is divided into paragraphs. You may not know that paragraphing can be used as a signal to redefine reading purposes as you read.

When an author begins a new paragraph he or she is saying, "Now I will begin talking about something different from the last paragraph." That "something different" might be a whole new topic, or just a different aspect of the same topic.

Sometimes you can tell what that new topic or subtopic will be. Sometimes the first sentence of a paragraph can be used as a signal to help you form a reading purpose to guide the reading of that paragraph.

Consider the list of sentences in Column A that follows. Each one should raise a question in your mind. Match each sentence with an appropriate question from Column B. Write your answers on a separate sheet of paper.

A. *Sentences*	B. *Questions Raised by Those Sentences*
1. They caught the ducks in an ingenious manner.	Why does the author say that? 4
2. This war was a turning point in Japan's history.	How did they do it? 1
3. One thing at least is very clear about late nineteenth-century workers.	What is it? 3
4. This proposal is obviously ridiculous.	What are they? 5
5. There are several possible explanations for the accident at the nuclear power plant.	Why was it? 2

Did the first sentence make you ask *how* they caught the ducks? Did the other sentences make you ask *why* the war was a turning point, *what is* clear about nineteenth-century workers, *why* the author says that the proposal is ridiculous, and *what are* the possible explanations for the accident?

Sentences like those in Column A are often found at the beginning of paragraphs. They raise questions that are then answered in the remainder of the paragraph. So those questions in Column B would be useful purposes to guide the reading of the paragraphs. Being alert for question-raising sentences like these is, therefore, one excellent strategy for redefining your reading purposes as you go along.

Suppose a paragraph begins with this sentence:

Contrary to the stereotype of the rabies'
victim foaming at the mouth, symptoms of
rabies are actually highly variable.

Will the rest of the paragraph deal with rabies' victims foaming at the mouth? What clue to idea relationships does the author use to signal the dismissal of this stereotype and a change in direction to something different? Look back at page 29 if necessary. What question should that sentence raise in your mind? Reader C found that sentence at the beginning of a paragraph in her magazine article. It gave her one of her reading purposes. Which one?

Sometimes the paragraph-opening sentence requires some untangling. Consider this paragraph-opening sentence:

> The government is currently spending twice as much as private industry on nuclear and solar research, but examination of past private and governmental research efforts suggests that we will get a much higher return from each private research dollar.

A careless reader might assume from the opening sentence that the rest of the paragraph will deal with the government's superior efforts in energy research. But, recalling the skill of untangling compound sentences, the careful reader would notice the comma followed by *but* and think this way: "There is a second core subject and verb in this sentence. The second message modifies or contrasts with the first part of the sentence in some way. The author is emphasizing the message following the *but*." So what question should guide reading of the rest of the paragraph?

A. Why does private industry get a far greater return from each research dollar?

B. Why is government more committed than private industry to energy research?

C. Why is private industry more committed than the government to energy research?

You probably had no trouble selecting A as the appropriate reading purpose question for this paragraph.

Try getting into the habit of pausing a moment over each paragraph-opening sentence. Think, "Does it raise some question? What direction does it signal for the rest of the paragraph?"

Sometimes you will come across a paragraph in which the first sentence seems to raise a question or announce a topic but then the rest of the paragraph goes on to develop something different. Does this mean it is unwise to use paragraph-opening sentences to form reading purposes? Must you first check to be sure that the paragraph-opening sentence is definitely the TOPIC SENTENCE of the paragraph, that is, that the remainder of the paragraph really does go on to develop the topic it announced?

No. The most important reason for using paragraph-opening sentences to form reading purposes is to keep your mind *actively involved* with the development of information in whatever you are reading. The actively involved mind is far more likely to be alert to sudden shifts in direction and to continue following the message of the text.

Sometimes a sentence at the end of one paragraph or at the beginning of the following paragraph signals a relationship between those two paragraphs. These signal sentences are TRANSITION SENTENCES. Suppose one paragraph ends:

> We gave each other a horrified look,
> rushed to the door, and threw it open.

What do you expect the next paragraph to be about?

    A. What was behind the door
    B. What they were doing in the house
    C. Who they were

A, of course.

Reader C of the rabies article found a paragraph that ended with this sentence:

The doctors compiled all this evidence and
issued a report that shocked the community.

It gave her one of her reading purposes. Which one?

The good reader is alert to sentences that signal, "This is what you are going to find out *next*." He or she must also be alert to sentences that signal, "This is what you should have *just learned*." Transition sentences often provide both these signals.

Suppose a new paragraph begins with this sentence:

Another example of the exercise of power by
Congress was the action taken by it during the
Reconstruction Period after the Civil War.

That sentence suggests what you should have learned from the preceding paragraph. What is it?

A. What Congress did during the Reconstruction Period
B. What Congress did before the Civil War
C. One example of Congress using its power

Did you pick C? Then you were right. When an author begins a paragraph saying *another example, another reason,* or *another opinion,* then you know that he or she has already given one example or reason or opinion.

Test yourself by saying, "Do I know what that first example was?" If you do, then you are ready to continue reading. Before you begin, use that same transition sentence to form a reading purpose for the next paragraph. What should you expect to find out in that paragraph?

A. The action Congress took during the Reconstruction Period
B. An example of Congress using its power after the Reconstruction Period
C. An example of Congress using its power during the Civil War

Did you pick A? Then you were right.

Now consider this transition sentence:

Johnson vigorously opposed these measures.

What should the reader have learned from the preceding paragraph?

A. Why Johnson opposed the measures
B. What the measures were
C. What Johnson did about it

The answer is B. Whenever an author begins a paragraph referring to *these measures, this rule,* or *those ideas,* you know the measures or rules or ideas were already stated in the preceding paragraph. Test yourself by asking, "Do I know what those measures are?" If you do, then you are ready to continue reading. But first, use the same transition sentence to form a purpose to guide your reading of the remainder of the paragraph. Which reading purpose is most appropriate?

A. "I will read to find out why Johnson opposed these measures."
B. "I will read to find out who had proposed these measures."
C. "I will read to find out what Johnson did to oppose these measures."

D. "I will read to find out about Johnson's opposition to these measures."

Although specific reading purposes are more useful than general ones, sometimes a reading purpose that is too specific can be misleading. Reread the transition sentence. Is reading purpose A possible? Yes. Is reading purpose C possible? Yes. You can't be sure yet just what aspect of Johnson's opposition the paragraph will develop. The careful reader would have formed purpose D.

Now think about this transition sentence:

Religion has undergone many changes in Massachusetts.

That sentence suggests what the reader should have learned from the preceding paragraph. Which of the following is it?

A. What these changes have been
B. What religion in Massachusetts was like before the change
C. What religion in Massachusetts will be like in the future

When an author begins a paragraph by mentioning *changes, improvements,* or *complications,* it is often true that he or she has just finished talking about the situation *before* those changes, improvements, or complications took place. Ask yourself, "Have I learned something about the background of religion in Massachusetts?" before continuing to read. (The answer above was B, of course.) Then use that transition sentence to make up a purpose to guide reading the remainder of the paragraph.

The ability to use transition sentences as signals in one or both of the two ways just described is so important that it is often tested in reading-comprehension exams. A PSAT exercise, for example, might look like this:

There are exceptions to the rule that seniority

should govern promotions, and some of these exceptions make sense.

The paragraph preceding this one probably

(1) discusses a principle governing advancement in business
(2) explains how factory workers are hired
(3) attacks mandatory retirement at age 65
(4) defends employer's right to discharge workers for inefficiency
(5) maintains that workers should evaluate their fellow workers

This transition sentence contains a signal word that functions much like the word *changes.* Identify that word below.

A. seniority
B. promotions
C. exceptions

When an author begins a new paragraph by mentioning an *exception to the rule,* it is likely that he or she has just finished talking about the rule itself. Now look back at choices 1 to 5. Which one must be correct? Choice 1, of course.

In this typical PSAT question, you need the whole paragraph to figure out how the final sentence suggests a reading purpose for the paragraph that will follow.

Starting our survey of the business cycle with the "prosperity phase," the key word is *growth.* Existing factories are enlarged. New plants, new transportation lines, new marketing centers are built. Demand for labor and raw materials rises. Prices rise and so do interest rates. Finally the spiral reaches a peak and the upward movement stops. The prosperity phase of the cycle is over.

The paragraph that follows is likely to deal with

(1) the causes of the prosperity phase
(2) the effect of prosperity on the standard of living
(3) the recession phase of the cycle
(4) indicators used to measure the business cycle
(5) attempts to avoid overexpansion

The paragraph given dealt with one phase of a cycle. What general statement can you make about that phase?

A. Things move up to a peak and finally stop.
B. Things move down from a peak and finally stop.

A, of course.

Since the author states in the final, transition sentence that he has finished talking about *one phase* of a cycle, what can you expect him to turn to next?

A. More characteristics of that phase
B. One of the groups discussed in the given paragraph
C. The next phase of the cycle

If you said C, you were right.

What do you suppose would be the direction of movement in this next phase? Look back at choices 1 to 5. Which one is a phase in which things move downward? Choice 3 is correct.

The greatest benefit of all these reading purpose strategies is that they force you to read *actively.* Too many readers expect to soak up information passively as their eyes move along the pages. The actively working reader who is involved with the development of events, facts, or ideas in what he or she is reading is the reader who comprehends and remembers more.

Chapter IV.
Keep Your Eye
on the Forest

You may be familiar with the old saying, "He couldn't see the forest for the trees." Which of these does it mean?

A. The forest was so densely overgrown that it was impossible to see more than a few trees.
B. He could not grasp the overall situation because he concentrated only on the details.

If you know that B is the correct meaning, then you probably understood the message of this chapter's title, "Keep Your Eye on the Forest." Keep your eye on the MAIN IDEAS in the material you read. They are what you are reading for; they are what you should remember. Don't become bogged down by details. Remember that details are included only to develop an author's main ideas.

To get the main idea of a paragraph you first need to know the topic of that paragraph. In Chapter III you worked with paragraphs in which the first sentence *announced* what the topic of the paragraph would be. But not all paragraphs begin with a topic sentence. Often the topic sentence is in the middle or at the end of the paragraph. Sometimes there is *no* sentence that states the topic. So, more often than not, you must recognize a "buried" topic sentence or make one up for yourself. To do so, you must know what all the sentences in the paragraph are about.

The first step in determining what *all* the sentences are about is to determine what *each individual* sentence is about. Try doing this with the sentences below. Write your answers on a separate sheet of paper.

Sentences	Topics
Jane is short.	This sentence is about Jane's ___High___.
Jane is thin.	This sentence is about Jane's ___size___.
Jane has blond hair.	This sentence is about Jane's ___hair___.

The topic of each sentence is different. But do these topics have anything in common? Of course they do. All the sentences are about what? Did you say they are all about Jane? This is true. But think back to a rule about reading purposes. To be most useful, a reading purpose should be as specific as possible. Similarly, to be most useful, the topic you select to tell what all the sentences in a paragraph are about must also be as specific as possible.

The topic *Jane* is too broad to sum up the topics of those three sentences. Having read them you still know nothing about Jane's age, personality, interests, family, etc. But you do have three pieces of information about the way Jane looks. All three sentences are about Jane's appearance. Could that topic be made still more specific? How about a narrower topic like *Jane's size*? Which sentence explains why this topic won't do?

A. It covers the topic *Jane's height* and *Jane's hair color,* but it does not cover the topic *Jane's weight.*
B. It covers the topic *Jane's height* and *Jane's weight,* but it does not cover the topic *Jane's hair color.*

Did you pick B? Then you see the principle: A topic must not be too broad, but it must be broad enough to include the topics of every individual sentence. The topic *Jane's size* is too narrow. So *Jane's appearance* is the topic of the three sentences.

You have just made up a topic that correctly covers three sentences and have arrived at the principle that governs paragraph topics. Now put that principle to work. Authors, you remember, often "bury" within a paragraph a sentence that states the topic of all the other sentences. Read the paragraph below. Can you recognize the sentence that states the topic of the paragraph?

The man in the next apartment can be heard *coughing* all night long through the thin wall that separates our apartments. The baby across the hall never seems to stop *crying,* day or night. At least once a night I am sure to hear the *screeching of sirens,* rushing toward some crisis in our neighborhood. As if all this weren't enough, a troupe of tuba players has taken to performing under my window every evening and their *music,* plus the *clapping* and *cheering* of their fans, now add to the overall volume. These are the *noises* I hear each night in my neighborhood.

To select the topic sentence, first determine the topic of each individual sentence (the italicized words should help here). From this list, is there a word that includes all the others? Which one?

coughing	clapping	screeching of sirens
noises	music	cheering
	crying	

Did you select *noises*? Then you were right, and you probably had no trouble selecting the paragraph's topic sentence, the one containing this overall word.

Once you have pinned down the topic of a paragraph you are ready to go on to the next step, the working out or identifying of a sentence that expresses the nub of what the author *said about* the topic, the main-idea sentence of the paragraph.

One strategy for recognizing a main-idea sentence is to determine, as you go along, the *function* served by each sentence in the paragraph. Look for a sentence that sounds like a "summing up"; this is likely to contain the main idea. A sentence that explains or gives an example or a piece of evidence or an argument is most likely supplying a detail that supports the main idea in some way. Such sentences are never main-idea sentences.

Here is a paragraph on which to try out the strategy just suggested. Read it through quickly and then work through the questions and explanations that follow it.

> Out of the Opium War came a treaty that was a landmark in China's history. It marked the beginning of the period in which China would have to deal with other nations on their terms rather than on its own terms. By treaty, Britain won the right to trade in five Chinese ports, not just the one port formerly allowed by the Chinese. British merchants could trade with anyone in those ports, not just with agents named by the Chinese government. British citizens could travel in limited areas around these ports, though this had previously been forbidden. And Britain was given possession of the Chinese island of Hong Kong. Seeing how well things had worked out for Britain, the United States, among other nations, sent representatives to China to obtain similar rights for themselves.

The first sentence recalls something you learned about in

Chapter III. Did you recognize that it is a transition sentence, providing a link between this paragraph and the one that preceded it in the textbook? Judging from this transition sentence, what do you think the paragraph preceding this one was about?

A. The Opium War
B. The provisions of the treaty

The war, of course. In providing a link between paragraphs, this transition sentence brings up a new topic: the treaty that was an outgrowth of the war. What question about this treaty does it raise?

A. Why was the treaty so important?
B. Which nations participated in the treaty?

The phrase *a landmark in China's history* should have alerted you to ask, "Why was it a landmark? Why was it so important?" Questions such as these should guide the reading of the paragraph.

The second sentence also deals with the treaty. Does it sound like a general "summing up" of the nature of the treaty? It could be the main-idea sentence, but only if the rest of the sentences in the paragraph support it in some way.

What is the topic of the third, fourth, and fifth sentences in the paragraph? What function do they serve?

A. They give examples of the provisions of the treaty.
B. They explain why China lost the Opium War.

If you selected A, then go on to think about each of those provisions. Does it sound as if they reflected what China wanted or what Britain wanted? In other words, do they support the idea that with this treaty China began having to deal with other nations on their terms rather than on its own? Yes. They are giving *examples* of specific ways in which China gave in to Britain's wishes. So the second sentence does express the main idea of the paragraph.

What function does the final sentence serve, A or B?

A. It provides another example to support the main idea.
B. It provides a transition to what will follow in the next paragraph.

Rather than provide more support for the main-idea sentence, this final sentence signals a change of direction for the paragraph to follow. Therefore the answer is B. What would you expect to read about in the paragraph that follows this one?

A. Further evidence of how well things worked out for Britain in China.
B. The United States' efforts to obtain similar rights.

You probably had little trouble selecting answer B.

Now consider this paragraph:

It was not newness that made the Declaration of Independence a great document. In fact the ideas that people have certain rights and that the purpose of government is to respect those rights were not new. They were the same ideas people had had from very early times. The idea that every human being had certain rights was generally accepted by educated Englishmen and by thoughtful people in many other countries of Europe. The great difference between the Declaration of Independence and other writings that said the same kinds of things was the idea that a government that did not protect those rights should be overthrown.

What is the topic of the opening sentence here? This sentence contains the *it-was-not* clue to idea relationships, signaling that one idea about the Declaration is being dismissed. What is that idea? That signal also alerts you to watch out for the *correct* statement about what made the Declaration great.

What are the second, third, and fourth sentences about? What function do they serve in the paragraph?

A. They explain what did make the Declaration of Independence great.
B. They give evidence to show why newness could not be what made the Declaration of Independence great.

All this *evidence* builds up the importance of the up-coming correct statement about what made the Declaration of Independence great. Does this statement appear in the paragraph? Yes. It is in the final sentence. Since the other sentences in the paragraph support this sentence, it is the main-idea sentence in the paragraph. Therefore B is correct.

You have practiced the strategy of identifying the main idea by asking yourself, "What is each sentence about?" and "What function does each sentence in the paragraph serve?" This strategy becomes even more important as we move on to paragraphs in which the author does not pull things together for you in a main-idea sentence. *You* have to identify the topic of the paragraph. You can do this by identifying the something-in-common of the sentences. Try doing this with the following paragraph:

Not too long ago a vacation meant time off from work in the summer. Now winter vacations are almost as popular. A vacation spent traveling abroad once involved a trip to well-known countries in

Europe. These days vacationing tourists often head for off-the-beaten-track corners of the globe. Going up the Amazon appeals to many of today's travelers as going down the Rhine once appealed to their grandparents.

Did you notice the topics *vacations in the past* and *vacations today*? Did you recognize the comparison being developed? What function do all the sentences here serve?

    A. They give examples of places you can go on your vacation.
    B. They give evidence concerning vacations today and vacations in the past.

The answer is B, of course.

    Although the paragraph does not provide a main-idea, summarizing sentence, you should have seen the point being developed by these "detail" sentences. Choose an appropriate main-idea sentence from the following:

    A. Vacations in the good old days were a lot more adventurous than vacations today.
    B. This is the way vacations were in the past and the way they are today.
    C. Vacations today are more varied than they used to be.

Which of those sentences best expresses the main idea of the paragraph? Sentence A? No. The idea it expresses is not supported by the evidence in the remainder of the paragraph. Sentence B? No. It just states the paragraph's topic without expressing any idea about it. Sentence C? Yes. C expresses the conclusion about vacations developed by the evidence in the other sentences of the paragraph.

    The next paragraph is a little more difficult because it

adds a new dimension to our concept of a main idea.

> In the living room of Beacon Lodge, chairs arranged in groups of different sizes made conversation easy. Well-placed lamps beside comfortable chairs insured that readers could be content. A blazing fire invited anyone coming in from the cold outdoors to forget the chill. Sunshine flooded the room by day; richly fashioned draperies closed out the darkness of night.

Deciding on the topic of this paragraph is easy. Each sentence describes some aspect of the physical appearance of the Beacon Lodge living room.

When four young people set out to write a main-idea sentence for this paragraph, all began with the words, *The living room of Beacon Lodge. . . .* Only one got to the heart of the matter though.

> Holly completed the sentence with
> the words *was very attractive.*
> Irwin wrote *was well furnished and comfortable.*
> Kate wrote *was attractive and inviting.*
> Joe wrote *had comfortable furniture
> and was well lighted and heated.*

By using the word *inviting,* Kate showed the greatest comprehension of the paragraph. Her sentence showed her awareness that each aspect of the room was described in terms that would attract people to use it. You can readily see why ability to express accurately and succinctly the main idea of what you read, as Kate did, is invaluable.

This skill, in fact, is considered so essential that it is heavily tested on reading comprehension exams. Most of the main-idea questions you meet ask you to choose, from a given list, the title for a paragraph or passage that best expresses the main idea. The description of Beacon Lodge, for example, might have been followed by this:

Choose the title that best expresses
the main idea of the passage.
      A. "Comfort at Beacon Lodge"
      B. "A Well-lighted Living Room"
      C. "A Well-planned Living Room"
      D. "A Room for Good Living"

How would you go about making your choice?

First, titles, like topics, should be neither too broad nor too narrow to sum up all the material they are meant to cover. Which choice does this eliminate right away? You probably saw that choice B is too narrow because the passage dealt with more than just the lighting in the room.

Kate's main-idea sentence illustrated another point that is true of titles too. They must catch the *flavor* of the passage. How does this help you zero in on the best title? Title C falls far short of expressing the flavor suggested by the details in the paragraph. Title A catches the spirit of some of the details—warmth on a cold day, comfortable chairs, good lighting. But there is something more than just physical comfort here. Activities encouraged by the room are mentioned, such as reading and conversing. Title D best expresses the main idea of this paragraph.

Now try a more difficult paragraph:

Some species, such as honeybees and stingless bees, communicate and act aggressively to acquire their energy resources. Others, like bumblebees, use individual initiative and foraging skill. In some bee species we see labor organization analogous to a Communist society; in others, division of labor results from a process like that described by Adam Smith for a capitalist society. In order to reconcile this diversity we have to examine each species in its own environment.

What is the topic of the first sentence? Which of the following is its function in the paragraph?

    A. It raises the question, "How do honeybees gather the pollen that supplies their energy resources?"
    B. It gives an example of how some species of bees get pollen.

Choice B is correct.

Which of the following are sentences two and three about? What function do they serve?

    A. They give examples of work patterns used by other species of bees to acquire pollen.
    B. They explain how bumblebees collect pollen.

Choice A is correct.

Which of the following is the function of the final sentence?

    A. It sums up the information presented in the preceding, detail sentences.
    B. It signals the direction that will be taken in the following paragraph or paragraphs.

You probably recognized that the final sentence was a transition sentence (choice B). Based on your understanding of this sentence, what do you expect to read about in the next paragraph?

    A. An examination of each species in its environment
    B. A summing up of all this evidence of diversity

(51)

Choice A is correct.

Consider the topics of all the sentences except the final, transition sentence. What do they have in common, A, B, or C?

    A. They all describe how bees make honey.
    B. They all discuss the bees' work patterns for gathering pollen.
    C. They all draw comparisons between the bees' work patterns and human work patterns.

Did you see that topic A is too broad and topic C is too narrow, but that B correctly states the something-in-common?

What main idea is the author expressing about these work patterns? Select from the following the title that best describes it.

    A. "Uniform Work Patterns for Gathering Pollen"
    B. "Diversity among Pollen Gatherers"
    C. "Varied Environments of Bee Societies"
    D. "How Bees Acquire Pollen"

Did you see that title C expresses an idea that was not developed in the paragraph? Did you recognize that title D merely stated the paragraph's topic but did not express any idea about that topic? Both A and B express ideas about the topic of the paragraph. But did you notice that the idea in A is exactly opposite to the point of the paragraph? Then you correctly selected title B.

Try finding the main idea in this passage:

Seriousness is not an attitude particular to poets. One can be serious about any subject—from pottery to publishing to putting to parenthood. Seriousness is simply the belief that some activity is more than a job or a pastime, that it is worth doing and doing well for some deeply felt and often inexpressible reason, and that that activity is worth thinking about.

There are people who take nothing seriously. They work to make a buck. They hack at pastimes. They may do what is expected. They may be competent workers or amiable companions, but they do not enlarge life by believing that some aspect of it is worth taking seriously.

Probably you easily recognized that all the sentences in the first paragraph are about the topic *seriousness.* By stating what seriousness is *not,* the first sentence raises the question, "Then what *is* seriousness?" The phrase *seriousness is not* also signals the reader to watch out for a correct statement of what seriousness *is.* Does that statement come in this paragraph? Yes. It is in the last sentence, which is the main-idea sentence of the first paragraph.

You probably also noted that all sentences in the second paragraph are about people who are not serious. What kinds of things does the writer say about them?

What main idea is the author developing here? Select the title from the following that best expresses the "flavor" of the passage:

A. "Toward a Better Understanding of Seriousness"
B. "In Defense of Seriousness"
C. "Seriousness—The Avoidable Obsession"
D. "How to Take Work and Play Seriously"

Did you notice the author's disdain for people who are not serious about anything? Then you probably got the flavor of the passage, a positive attitude toward seriousness, and realized that title C expresses the opposite attitude. And you also eliminated title A because it misses the passage's positive attitude. Did you note that title D was not dealt with in the passage? Then you correctly chose title B.

As a final test of your ability to work with main ideas, here is a more difficult paragraph. Read it carefully.

(1) Although they will be expensive, synthetic fuels are a crucial part of our energy plans because they can fill the relatively small gap between supply and demand for oil that is anticipated in the 1980s. (2) It is a common misconception that the power of the Organization of Petroleum Exporting Countries (OPEC) comes from its huge volume of oil production, but actually OPEC's power lies in its ability to hold back just enough oil from the market to dictate prices. (3) Most OPEC countries are limited in this ability to cut back, however, because they need the money their oil brings in. (4) If use of synthetic fuels could reduce our demand for OPEC's oil by just one-sixth, OPEC's stranglehold on world oil prices would be sharply curtailed.

You may need to use the sentence untangling strategy (introduced in Chapter I) to get the message in the first sentence. Did you find out why synthetic fuels are a crucial part of our energy plans?

Sentence (2) begins with a negative statement that signals dismissal of an incorrect idea about what gives OPEC its power. It says this power does *not* come from the huge volume of oil production. The *correct* statement about the source of OPEC's power is in the same sentence. Did you find it?

In Sentence (3) did you find out the limit to OPEC's power?

Did you use the sentence untangling strategy with Sentence (4)? Did you find how a small reduction in demand would help the oil importing nations?

If you found the answers to these questions then you should see what the something-in-common of all the sentences is. This something-in-common will lead you to the main idea these sentences develop. Did you find these answers?

> *Sentence (1).* Synthetic fuels are a crucial part of our energy plans because they could fill a small gap between supply and demand for oil.
> *Sentence (2).* OPEC's power is its ability to dictate the price of oil by lowering the supply even by a small amount.
> *Sentence (3).* Most OPEC members can afford to cut back their contribution to the supply of oil by only a small amount.
> *Sentence (4).* A small decrease in demand for oil would give purchasing countries a greater influence over price.

Did you see that each sentence has something to do with a *small* change in the supply or demand for oil? All the sentences help to *explain* the importance of this small change. The paragraph contains no sentence that pulls together the idea these sentences are developing. But the reader should be able to follow the development and get the main idea.

Which title do you think best expresses the main idea of this paragraph?

A. "The Rolling Stone That Gathers Much Moss"
B. "The Tail That Could Wag the Dog"
C. "The Light at the End of the Tunnel"
D. "The Mouse That Roared"
E. "The Mighty Oaks That Grow from Acorns"

Did you pick title B? Then you were right.

Chapter V.
Take Tests in Stride

If you can untangle complicated sentences and follow the idea relationships in and among sentences and paragraphs, then you will have a better than average level of reading comprehension. If you can recognize or express the main ideas in a piece of reading material, and if you read actively and are guided by purpose, you will have less difficulty reading homework assignments and answering questions about them.

A different kind of challenge is presented by tests specifically designed to evaluate your reading competence. For many people these tests are very high hurdles indeed. Time limits can make the test-taker feel anxious. Awareness of the importance of doing well also increases the tension, and the questions themselves seem foreign, unfamiliar. They probe aspects of reading comprehension that day-to-day schoolwork and free-time reading rarely test.

You have met many samples of such questions in this book. They were included to demonstrate the usefulness of the specific reading strategies being taught. In this final chapter we will do two things: (1) introduce three additional types of questions that appear over and over on standardized tests, and (2) suggest some test-taking strategies.

Here is a passage followed by questions based on it

that is typical of what you might face on, say, a PSAT test. Do not try to answer the questions after you have read the passage. Just briefly look them over, and then go on with your reading of the regular text.

(1) The typical tennis player out to buy equipment for the game brings little expertise to the selection process. A little comparison of prices, some pondering over the "feel" of this racquet versus the "feel" of that one, and the purchase is made—the racquet that will make him or her another Tilden.

(2) A less casual approach to racquets has been taken by one tennis playing physicist. Intrigued by the dynamics of ball and racquet action, he decided to go beyond obvious differences and get some hard facts about the relationship between a tennis racquet's construction and its performance.

(3) He soon found that the location of the center of percussion varied from racquet to racquet. When a tennis ball is hit at a right angle by the percussion center of a racquet, it will travel in a precise, one hundred eighty degree straight line. A hit away from this "sweet spot"—to use tennis players' jargon— may go right or left, long or short, of its intended placement. Only in larger-frame racquets was the "sweet spot" found near the center of the racquet head, the best place for it.

(4) Other factors involved in the seemingly simple act of hitting a tennis ball came under study. Using the delicate instruments of the physicist it was possible to measure how long the ball stayed in contact with the strings (the dwell time) and how long it took the racquet head to bend and return when hit (the oscillation period). These two factors affect the

speed of a return. Comparison of the data for many racquets led to the conclusion that stiffer racquets would mean more powerful shots.

(5) Further studies, this time of racquet stringing, convinced the investigator that tensions lower than the forty-five to sixty pound range he found would make for better racquet response.

(6) Students who take physics with this tennis playing professor reap the benefit of all these investigations in a lecture devoted entirely to the subject— the dynamics of the tennis racquet.

1. The best title for this article would be

    (A) "Using Physics to Improve Your Tennis Game"
    (B) "The Science Behind the Shots"
    (C) "How To Make Better Tennis Racquets"
    (D) "A Sports-loving Scientist at Work"
    (E) "Tennis—A Game for Physicists"

2. According to this article, tennis racquets differ in (1) size of frame (2) tension of strings (3) location of percussion center (4) length of handle:

    (A)   None of the above.
    (B)   One of the above.
    (C)   Two of the above.
    (D)   Three of the above.
    (E)   All of the above.

3. Which statement is true, according to the passage?

    (A)   Hitting a tennis ball is easy if you have a large enough racquet.
    (B)   The dwell time is known to physicists as the oscillation period.

(C) A ball hit on the percussion center is likely to go where the player intended.

(D) You can hit a ball coming at you only if you get your racquet at right angles to it.

(E) "Sweet spot" means tennis players' jargon.

4. The word *dynamics,* as used in the second and last paragraphs, means

(A) forces affecting motion
(B) ratios of oscillation
(C) measures of speed
(D) explosive qualities
(E) playing styles

5. The passage implies that Tilden, mentioned in the first paragraph, was

(A) the creator of the modern tennis racquet
(B) a great tennis player
(C) a well-known sports commentator
(D) a manufacturer of tennis racquets
(E) the tennis playing physicist whose work is described

Which should you read first, the passage or the questions? You should read the passage, by all means. But it must be a quick, once-over-lightly reading, in which you put to use your ability to recognize what a paragraph is *about.*

Whip through the first paragraph and make a mental note—it's about buying tennis equipment; second paragraph—about someone who is studying tennis racquets; third paragraph—about percussion centers (don't try to get details here). Fourth paragraph opens with our old friend, a transition sentence. *Other factors* are coming, so percussion centers must have been the first factor that enters into the hitting of the ball. Fifth paragraph—racquet stringing; sixth paragraph—sign off.

Now you are ready to look at the questions. This first look should not be a slow, careful work-through. You should read just the stem of each question—the part of the question that precedes the choices. You see a best-title question, a definition question, two that obviously are going to require a close look at details, plus an inference question.

Which one should you do first? You know you can't do the best-title question until you have finished your second, more thorough reading. Does one question seem easier to you than another? Do it first. Does one look very difficult? Try something else first. If you have no favorite, take a good look at Question 2.

The question deals with differences among racquets. You know there was no whole paragraph on this topic. So you must track down each of the subtopics listed in the stem of the question. Having located where each subtopic is discussed, read carefully to see whether anything about differences is explicitly stated.

You remember from your first quick reading where *stringing* is talked about, so go straight to paragraph 5. Read it carefully now. Is there anything about differences? Untangling the first sentence, as you learned to do in Chapter I, you identify *studies* and *convinced* as core subject and core verb. "Studies of what?" you ask yourself. "String tensions lower than what?" Pinning down the answer to your second question you see that racquets have a *forty-five to sixty pound range.* If there is a *range* of tension among racquets, they differ. So subtopic (2) should be checked.

You know where percussion centers are talked about, so go next to paragraph 3. In the very first sentence you see what you need. Subtopic (3) should be checked. Read the rest of the paragraph to see if there is anything about size of frames or length of racquet handles. Sure enough, the last sentence refers to *larger frames,* so subtopic (1) is also correct.

Subtopic (4) is tricky. So far in the paragraphs you have

read carefully there has been no mention of this. You may know that the lengths of racquet handles vary, but the question, remember, says *according to the article.* So don't choose or reject (4) until you have finished rereading all of the paragraphs. (Actually you will find no mention of handle length, so the correct answer to Question 2 is D.)

Question 3 samples the same reading-comprehension skill as did Question 2, that is, the ability to find answers to questions when the answers are given in the material.

In order to check out the accuracy of the first statement you must go to the places where hitting is talked about. There was no whole paragraph on this topic, so you must skim to find that word, wherever it occurs. Rereading paragraph 3 shows nothing that suggests whether the hits mentioned are easy or difficult, so move on. In the first line of the fourth paragraph you find a clue in the word *seemingly.* When the writer calls hitting a ball *seemingly simple,* it is an abbreviated way of saying: "It only seems simple, but it is not." So choice (A) is clearly not true.

To check out choice (B) you go to the *other factors* paragraph. Using what you learned in Chapter II about given definitions, you know exactly what *dwell time* and *oscillation period* are. You recognize (B) as an attempt to trick you.

To check choice (C) you again go back to paragraph 3. Here you pin down the detail that the percussion center is the *sweet spot.* You are explicitly told that a right-angle hit on the *sweet spot* will travel in a 180-degree—hence straight —line. This makes choice (C) very attractive, but the remaining choices should be checked out to be sure.

The same words that seem to verify choice (C) tend to eliminate choice (D). *When a tennis ball is hit at a right angle.* . . . certainly does not say that you cannot touch it at all at any other angle.

Choice (E) is what is sometimes called a "nonsense foil." It makes no sense but might fool the careless. The careful reader knows, again from Chapter II, that the words this "sweet spot" signaled that the meaning of *sweet spot* was in the preceding words. The phrase within the dashes simply added the information that the term *sweet spot* is part of the special vocabulary of tennis players. With choices (A), (B), (D), and (E) proved inaccurate, the hunch that choice (C) is correct is verified.

Question 4 is a typical definition question. One way to handle it is to substitute each of the answer choices in places where the word occurs. Some substitutions make no sense and can be eliminated. For example, when you substitute *ratios of oscillation* for *dynamics* in the last paragraph, it makes no sense. A whole lecture would not be devoted to those ratios; they were mentioned only in connection with *dwell time,* a detail in paragraph 4. Substituting *measures of speed* makes just as little sense. Speed was just one of the many details of tennis-racquet performance talked about. *Playing styles* won't do. Players have playing styles, not tennis racquets. How about *explosive qualities*? This is a nonsense foil, similar to the one you met earlier. It makes no sense, but some careless test-taker might make a foolish connection between dynamics and dynamite. *Forces affecting motion* makes sense, and you know that the whole passage was about what makes tennis balls move as they do. So choice (A) is the correct answer.

Now we must tackle Question 5. If you know who Tilden was, this question is no problem at all. If you don't, Question 5 forces you to make an *inference.* When you make an inference you must combine some information given you with some information you already know.

How can you make an inference on the Tilden question? Well, you are *given the information* that if you are an average tennis player you hope your racquet will make you another Tilden. You *know* that average players of any game aspire to be like the greats in their game. Thus (inference), Tilden must have been a great tennis player. Choice (B) is correct.

Having worked through the tennis passage to answer

Questions 2 to 5, we finally go back to Question 1, the best-title question. This kind of question, you recall from Chapter IV, tests your ability to get the main ideas and flavor of a paragraph or passage. Using the principles you learned in that chapter you eliminate choices (D) and (E) as too broad. Choices (A) and (C) have the wrong flavor. Obviously the article is not intended to improve anyone's tennis game. It is not addressed to sporting-goods manufacturers, although they might well find it useful. Clearly the writer is focusing on the scientific explanations for the behavior of tennis racquets and tennis balls. Choice (B) reflects this.

MORE ABOUT
INFERENCE QUESTIONS

Many questions test the reader's ability to make an inference. Making inferences may sound like a difficult and sophisticated reading-comprehension skill, and it is. But here is a way that may help you to better deal with inferences.

Sherlock Holmes made his reputation as a detective by his ability to make inferences. He could take a piece of evidence like this:

Footprints near a house that had been robbed

add to it something he knew from his education or experience:

The depth of a footprint varies with
the bulk of the person who makes it

and come up with the observation—the sophisticated word for this is *deduction*—that:

The thief was a heavyset person.

Again, an inference requires two things:

Information PLUS Information from
given your background
of knowledge and
experience

Every time you laugh at a cartoon you are making an inference. This cartoon, for example, would not be funny unless
you bring to it your knowledge that a movement is underway
to shift to the metric system. The shift *would* mean measur-
ing milk in litres, and you enjoy the absurdity of cows ad-
justing their thinking to conform to ours.

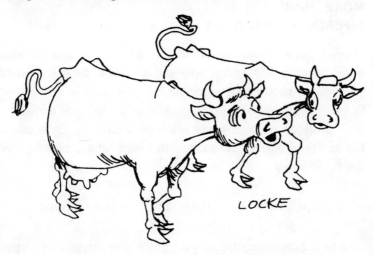

LOCKE

"You been switched to litres yet,
or are you still giving quarts?"

Here is another inference question. You are given this:

It is the cost of getting oil
out of the ground that keeps
some of it from being tapped.

This statement implies which of the following?

  (A) Some oil is buried too deep to be reached.
  (B) Higher prices for oil would make new wells profit-
      able.
  (C) Getting more oil out of the ground would cut its
      cost.
  (D) People will not buy oil that costs too much.
  (E) It costs a great deal to produce oil.

To make the correct inference you must bring to the given sentence the following information from your general background:

•   Oil in hard-to-reach places costs more to produce than oil that is easy to get at.
•   Businesses won't produce something unless they can sell it for more than it costs to produce.

If you have this information you can readily see that choice (B) is a reasonable inference.

In another kind of inference question, you must supply the meaning of a term used in the question. Here is a reading-test passage with a typical inference question based on it.

The gross national product (GNP) of a country is watched as an indicator of the health of a country's economy. In time of war, tanks and planes may be produced instead of automobiles or washing machines; lumber may go to build barracks instead of houses. People find fewer goods in the stores. But the gross national product rises sharply.

This passage implies that the GNP

(A) does not include household goods.
(B) becomes inaccurate in wartime.
(C) may be a poor indicator of living conditions.
(D) measures a country's standard of living.
(E) ignores consumer goods.

You can answer this question only if you know what the GNP is. In other words, what you must bring to the question is the definition of a term the examiners think you should know.

Information given	*You bring*
GNP going up at a time when available consumer goods are going down	• You know that the GNP is the value of the goods and services produced in, say, a year.
	• You know that living conditions depend on whether consumers can buy what they need.

You reason that if the GNP can go up when consumers are having a hard time buying what they need, then the GNP does not give a good picture of what is happening to living conditions. So the only possible inference is choice (C).

Some reading-comprehension questions phrased as inference questions require a different skill. This skill is the ability to recognize a *paraphrase*. A paraphrase is a statement of the sense of a sentence, paragraph, or passage.

Here is a typical inference question that tests the ability to recognize paraphrasing.

People have always been aware of the usefulness of high places as "watchout places." Years ago frontier scouts climbed hills from which they could look for signs of Indian activity. Seashore communities build lighthouse towers whose beacons serve as warning signals to ships at sea. Forest rangers know that there is no substitute, in their fire prevention system, for a chain of watchtowers. The "high places" created by space technology nowadays make possible observation of almost anything, anywhere.

This paragraph implies that

    (A) Lighthouses eliminate accidents at sea.
    (B) Beacons are special sea patrols.
    (C) Human conquest of the air means an ability to control air pollution.
    (D) Low places are of little value.
    (E) Observation is essential to forest-fire prevention.

The correct answer, choice (E), can be arrived at by matching words in the passage with paraphrases of those words in the choices:

there is no substitute in the paragraph is paraphrased as *essential* in choice (E).
a chain of watchtowers in the paragraph is paraphrased as *observation* in choice (E).

Now, a last word.
    Sometimes reading is work. Sometimes it is recreation. Always, however, it involves interaction between the reader and the printed page.
    This book has tried to suggest the kinds of interaction between reader and words that improve comprehension. If you use these suggestions, if you work at being an active, thinking, *good* reader, you will reap a bonus benefit. You will discover, if you did not already know it, that reading can be great fun!

Index

Action words, 3, 4, 7, 11, 12, 13

But signal, 7, 8, 10, 11, 20, 25

Chapters and chapter headings, 30–31
Commas, 3, 6, 7, 8, 10, 11, 34
Core subject, 1–14, 34
Core verb, 1–14, 34

Dashes, 11, 12, 16
Definition question, 62
Definitions, 15–17
Detail sentences, 48, 49, 50

Exception to the rule, 39

Graphics, 31, 32

Homework, 26, 56

Idea relationships, 20–25, 47, 56
Illustrations, 31
Inference questions, 62–66
-ing words, 4, 10

Main ideas, 41–55
Maps, 31, 32

Negative statement, 23, 54

Paragraph topic, 41–44, 47–49, 52

Paragraph-opening sentence, 33–39
Paraphrasing, 66–67
Parentheses, 16
Pronouns, 7–8, 12, 13
PSAT, 38, 39
Punctuation, 2, 3, 11, 16, 34

Question-raising sentence, 33–35
Questions, 62–66

Reading-comprehension tests, 24, 38, 49, 56–67
Reading purposes, 26–40

Semicolons, 11
Sentence patterns, 6–11
Sentence topics, 42, 47, 51, 52
Sentence-untangling strategy, 1–14
Sequence relationships, 17–20
State-of-being verbs, 3–7, 11–13
Summing-up sentence, 44, 45, 51

Tests, 24, 38, 49, 56–67
Textbooks, 2, 23, 26, 30, 31, 32
Time relationships, 17–20
Titles and headings, 30, 31, 49–55
Topics and topic sentences, 35, 41–48, 52, 53
Transition sentences, 35–40, 45, 51, 52

Word meanings, 15–17